‖‖ ‖ ‖‖‖‖ ‖ ‖‖ ‖‖‖‖‖‖‖‖‖ ‖ ‖‖ ‖
W9-BOO-210

B
GEORGE

Gaines, Ann.

King George III.

$18.95

13BT03401

DATE			

D E GAVIT JR SR HIGH SCHOOL
1670 175TH STREET
HAMMOND, IN 46324

BAKER & TAYLOR

King George III

English Monarch

Colonial Leaders

Lord Baltimore
English Politician and Colonist

Benjamin Banneker
American Mathematician and Astronomer

Sir William Berkeley
Governor of Virginia

William Bradford
Governor of Plymouth Colony

Jonathan Edwards
Colonial Religious Leader

Benjamin Franklin
American Statesman, Scientist, and Writer

Anne Hutchinson
Religious Leader

Cotton Mather
Author, Clergyman, and Scholar

Increase Mather
Clergyman and Scholar

James Oglethorpe
Humanitarian and Soldier

William Penn
Founder of Democracy

Sir Walter Raleigh
English Explorer and Author

Caesar Rodney
American Patriot

John Smith
English Explorer and Colonist

Miles Standish
Plymouth Colony Leader

Peter Stuyvesant
Dutch Military Leader

George Whitefield
Clergyman and Scholar

Roger Williams
Founder of Rhode Island

John Winthrop
Politician and Statesman

John Peter Zenger
Free Press Advocate

Revolutionary War Leaders

John Adams
Second U.S. President

Ethan Allen
Revolutionary Hero

Benedict Arnold
Traitor to the Cause

King George III
English Monarch

Nathanael Greene
Military Leader

Nathan Hale
Revolutionary Hero

Alexander Hamilton
First U.S. Secretary of the Treasury

John Hancock
President of the Continental Congress

Patrick Henry
American Statesman and Speaker

John Jay
First Chief Justice of the Supreme Court

Thomas Jefferson
Author of the Declaration of Independence

John Paul Jones
Father of the U.S. Navy

Lafayette
French Freedom Fighter

James Madison
Father of the Constitution

Francis Marion
The Swamp Fox

James Monroe
American Statesman

Thomas Paine
Political Writer

Paul Revere
American Patriot

Betsy Ross
American Patriot

George Washington
First U.S. President

Famous Figures of the Civil War Era

Jefferson Davis
Confederate President

Frederick Douglass
Abolitionist and Author

Ulysses S. Grant
Military Leader and President

Stonewall Jackson
Confederate General

Robert E. Lee
Confederate General

Abraham Lincoln
Civil War President

William Sherman
Union General

Harriet Beecher Stowe
Author of Uncle Tom's Cabin

Sojourner Truth
Abolitionist, Suffragist, and Preacher

Harriet Tubman
Leader of the Underground Railroad

King George III

English Monarch

Ann Graham Gaines

Arthur M. Schlesinger, jr.
Senior Consulting Editor

Chelsea House Publishers

Philadelphia

Produced by 21st Century Publishing and Communications, Inc.
New York, NY. http://www.21cpc.com

CHELSEA HOUSE PUBLISHERS
Production Manager Pamela Loos
Art Director Sara Davis
Director of Photography Judy L. Hasday
Managing Editor James D. Gallagher
Senior Production Editor J. Christopher Higgins

Staff for *KING GEORGE III*
Project Editor/Publishing Coordinator Jim McAvoy
Project Editor Anne Hill
Associate Art Director Takeshi Takahashi
Series Design Keith Trego

©2001 by Chelsea House Publishers, a subsidiary of Haights Cross
Communications. All rights reserved. Printed and bound in the
United States of America.

The Chelsea House World Wide Web address is
http://www.chelseahouse.com

First Printing
1 3 5 7 9 8 6 4 2

Library of Congress Cataloging-in-Publication Data

Gaines, Ann.
 King George III / Ann G. Gaines.
  p. cm. — (Revolutionary War leaders)
 Includes bibliographical references and index.
 ISBN 0-7910-5978-2 (hc) — 0-7910-6136-1 (pbk.)
 1. George III, King of Great Britain, 1738–1820—Juvenile literature.
 2. Great Britain—History—George III, 1738–1820—Juvenile literature.
 3. Great Britain—Kings and rulers—Biography—Juvenile literature.
 [1. George III, King of Great Britain, 1738–1820. 2. Kings, queens,
 rulers, etc.] I. Title. II. Series.

DA506.A2.G27 2000
941.07'3'092—dc21
 [B]   00-038386
                                                            CIP

Publisher's Note: In Colonial and Revolutionary War America,
there were no standard rules for spelling, punctuation, capitaliza-
tion, or grammar. Some of the quotations that appear in the Colonial Leaders and Revolutionary War Leaders series come from
original documents and letters written during this time in history.
Original quotations reflect writing inconsistencies of the period.

Contents

George was born in London. The young prince knew that one day he would be the king of his country. He worked hard to prepare himself for the big responsibility.

The Young Prince

King George III of England ruled his country for nearly 60 years. His position gave him large estates of land. He had great amounts of money and a lot of power. He was very proud of being a proper king for his people. But his life was also filled with great sadness.

On June 4, 1738, George William Frederick was born. He was a premature baby–born two months early. Most of those present at his birth thought that the weak and tiny infant would not survive. So he was **baptized** that very night.

Baby George belonged to a very important

family. He was the grandson of King George II. His father, Frederick Lewis, would become king when George II died.

George III's family came to England from Germany. His great-grandfather was King George I. George I had lived in a small state in Germany called Hanover. When Queen Anne of England died in 1714, George I was next in line to be king. He moved to England in 1707.

King George I took his grown-up son George II with him. But he ordered his seven-year-old grand-son Frederick Lewis to stay in Hanover.

Frederick Lewis grew

In 1235, a family named Welf became the rulers of the tiny German country of Hanover. The Welf family later became known as the Hanovers. They ruled the tiny country for hundreds of years.

In 1658, Duke Ernest Augustus of Hanover married Sophia. She was the grand-daughter of King James I of England. Duke Ernest died in 1698. Their oldest son, George Louis, became the elector of Hanover.

In 1714, George Louis became King George I of England. He moved to the new country he had to rule. His family, the Hanovers, reigned over England from 1714 to 1901.

up and was educated in Hanover. He was apart from his father and grandfather for 13 years. Finally, when Frederick Lewis was 21 years old, George I let him move to England, even though he had not yet learned English.

The very next year, old King George I died. That made George II the king of England. Frederick Lewis became the new Prince of Wales. (The Prince of Wales is the title given to the oldest son of the king or queen of England. The prince is the next in line to rule when the current king or queen dies.)

After a while, King George II chose a wife for his son Frederick Lewis. Her name was Augusta and she came from a powerful family. Her father was the duke of Saxe-Gotha, another German state. Augusta was only 17 when she came to England to marry Frederick. She did not speak English either.

Frederick Lewis and Augusta had a baby girl in 1737. They named her Augusta, after her mother. George William Frederick was born next. In spite of being a prematurely born and extremely weak baby, George lived. He would become the king after his grandfather and father.

George's father loved his family. He and his wife had nine children.

The royal couple was popular in London high society and frequently had visitors. There must have always been someone for young Prince George to play with. The family often entertained itself by going to see the royal children and their friends put on plays at **court**.

Prince George made friends with a boy six years older than he was. The boy's name was Frederick North. North played roles in the royal plays too. His father was an **earl**.

George didn't go to school. He had **tutors** instead. They were special teachers hired to teach only George and his younger brother Prince Edward. George learned his alphabet, in both German and English.

George's father and mother did not get along very well with his grandfather, King

George's grandfather, King George II, was the last British king to lead troops into battle.

George II. King George II couldn't always do everything he wanted to do. He had to deal with **Parliament**, England's legislature. Young George's father had taken sides with the king's enemies in Parliament. This made the king very mad at his son.

One day, George's father caught a cold. No

In 1750, the king of England was given about a million pounds a year to meet his expenses—a huge amount of money. At that time, 150 pounds would pay the year's bills for the family of a doctor. A day-laborer's family would live on less than 40 pounds a year. A rich merchant might make 10,000 pounds a year.

The king got paid 100 times what a rich merchant earned. But sometimes even that much money was not enough. Then the king had to ask Parliament to pay his extra bills. Sometimes Parliament refused.

one thought much about it because everyone gets colds sometimes. But the Prince of Wales did not get better. On March 20, 1751, he died. George's father was only 44 years old.

George was only 12 at the time of his father's death. But he didn't have time to feel sad because he had a new job for which he needed to prepare. George became the new Prince of Wales and would become king when his grandfather King George II died.

King George II was nearly 68 years old. Everyone kept reminding George that he could become king at any moment. And the prince wouldn't just be king of one small country. Great Britain controlled land all over the world, which

**George (right) with his brother Edward Augustus.
The boys did not go to school but had special
teachers who taught them at the palace.**

together formed the British **Empire**. Thinking
about what a big job governing that empire
would be made George become a serious young
man. He spent more time learning from, and talking to, adults. They tried to help George learn
everything he'd need to know to be a good king.

John Stuart, George's tutor. When George became king, Stuart became his trusted advisor.

After his father's death, George's mother took charge of his education. Princess Augusta asked John Stuart for help. He was the third earl of Bute and his family came from Scotland. The Princess encouraged Lord Bute to take a personal interest in the formal education of her son. John Stuart agreed and became George's tutor. George and his new tutor soon became very good friends.

Prince George was determined to be as good a ruler as any English man or woman had been before him. He studied hard to find out what English kings and queens had done in the past. He also learned what they hadn't done.

The young prince was also taught by other tutors who were chosen by Lord Bute. By the time he was 17, George knew French, German, Latin, and Greek. He also had a general knowledge of world history, science, and math, as well as drawing and military defenses. He began a life-long interest in observing the stars and planets, and learned about the teachings and ceremonies of the Anglican Church.

His education included lessons in many of the

social activities of the time, such as dancing, fencing, riding, and music. Young George learned to play the harpsichord and the flute, and had an interest in art and architecture. George loved learning, and most of all, he loved his books.

Prince George received an exceptional education—better than the best schools in England could provide. But during the years after his father died, he did not play with other boys. He knew nothing firsthand of what life was like for those who lived outside the court. Dealing only with adults left him serious and perhaps a bit stuffy and overly proud.

When George turned 18, his 73-year-old grandfather, King George II, gave him a birthday present: an annual income of 40,000 pounds, a truly princely sum. George II also told the future king he would pay for him to have his own separate house.

The prince asked the king to buy him a house next door to his mother's house. He had been happy at home and would be glad to be near his mother to continue their close relationship.

Four years later, George's life changed again. Early on the morning of October 25, 1760, King George II got out of bed and, on his way to the bathroom, suddenly fell over. A doctor was called to the king's rooms, and the king was pronounced dead. His death had come swiftly. There had been no warning signs.

George was setting out for his morning ride when he received a note from Princess Amelia informing him that the king was dead. In an instant, the prince became King George III. He was only 22.

As soon as he received the news, George returned to his home. There, he wrote a note to Lord Bute, asking his teacher what he should do next. The older man kindly advised the new king.

First, the old king had to be buried. After those ceremonies were over, King George III settled down to business. He asked Lord Bute to be one of his important advisors.

George knew that one of a king's jobs was to

George at the time he became Prince of Wales. That title meant he was next in line to become king.

make sure he had sons to take over when he died. The new king knew he needed to get married and have a family.

Before he died, King George II had let it be known that he wished his grandson would find a

German princess to marry. Germany was made up of a number of small states. Almost every one of those states had **noble** families with daughters waiting to get married. Any of those young girls would be glad to marry the king of England and the ruler of all Britain.

George II had not chosen his grandson's wife. He left the choice up to the young prince. A few months after the old king died, George asked Lord Bute to make a list of all the eligible women in Germany he might marry. The new king asked his old teacher to report on the strengths and weaknesses of each of the girls.

George did not pay much attention to what the girls looked like. He wanted to find a good companion and mother for his future children. He finally chose Charlotte Sophia, of Mecklenburg. They were married on September 8, 1761.

Two weeks after the wedding, on September 22, 1761, George and his bride took part in an important ceremony. At 11 o'clock in the morning, dressed in regal attire, they left the castle in sedan chairs.

For two hours, they were carried through the streets of London on their way to Westminster Abbey. (The abbey is the **cathedral** of the Church of England in London.) Crowds lined the entire route to see the royal couple. Once the newlyweds reached the abbey, they took part in a formal ceremony called a coronation. The ceremony went on for more than two hours. A choir sang, men read from the Bible, and prayers were said.

Finally, after three o'clock in the afternoon, George was crowned king and his wife was crowned Queen Charlotte. George's official title was very long. It was King George III, King of Great Britain and Ireland, Duke and Elector of Hanover, Duke of Cornwall and Rothesay, Duke of Edinburgh, Marquess of Ely, Earl of Etham, Viscount of Launceston, Baron of Snowdon, and Earl of Chester.

King George III made a promise called the

Oath of Coronation. He swore to protect the rights and privileges of the Church of England. That oath was very important to George. "Where is that power on earth to absolve me from the due observance of every sentence of that oath?" he asked. "I had rather beg my bread from door to door throughout Europe than consent to any such measure."

After the solemn ceremony, the king and queen threw a huge party. They invited all the important people. Lots of food covered the tables. People stayed until after 10 o'clock that night. Only then did the king and queen return to St. James Palace to go to bed.

Even after he became a king, George preferred life in the country. He liked farming so much that he was called "Farmer George."

2

The Royal Family

King George III and Queen Charlotte had many duties. Their jobs had to be done in the city of London. But most of the time, they lived about 10 miles from London.

Their home was named Kew. It was a huge estate with 120 acres of land. The grounds were beautiful. George had grown up at Kew and liked living in his parents' old home.

Meanwhile, Queen Charlotte had her eye on another castle about 20 miles from London—Windsor Castle. It had been the favorite home of kings of England since William the Conqueror in

1066. In 1775, Queen Charlotte asked for and was given Windsor Castle.

The royal lands were near the village of Windsor. They included a castle, several farms, open meadows, and woods. The castle had been empty and Queen Charlotte worked to fix it up.

The king and queen came to live there more and more. They lived a simple country life. King George spoke openly with everyone who lived in the village. He was proud to be an English gentleman, as well as the king of all Great Britain.

He was given more than a million pounds a year by the English people. That was a huge amount of money. The king used the money to pay for the upkeep on several castles. He also paid for homes for himself and his family in London and other cities.

Then there were all the bills for running his farms and estates throughout England, Ireland, Wales, and Scotland. He also had to pay the expenses for his supporters in the government.

The House of Commons. Although Great Britain had a population of more than 8 million people, only 215,000 men had the right to vote.

Earls and dukes with lots of money inherited seats in the **House of Lords**–Parliament's upper house. But members of the lower house–the **House of Commons**–were elected. Some years, George spent 200,000 pounds in order to get candidates he liked elected. These were the people he could count on to vote as he wished them to.

Over the years, King George III and Queen Charlotte had 15 children. There were nine sons and six daughters. The two youngest boys died when they were very young.

George was in charge of how the boys were brought up. A strict but loving parent, he modeled their education on his own. He felt that the strict upbringing he had received had been a good one for someone with royal duties and obligations.

The boys' general schedule was the same as their father's had been when he was a boy. Servants woke them by 7:30 in the morning and the boys arrived in their schoolroom half an hour later. From then until eight o'clock at night, they were under the direction of tutors, with time out only for lunch and a period of exercise. Every other day, they were also allowed one hour for play. Sunday was a day of rest. The children attended church and a formal reception at the castle. They also

King George, Queen Charlotte, and 6 of their children. George was a strict but loving father to his 15 children.

received religious instruction.

George loved his sons but felt uncomfortable with them and greatly preferred to be with his daughters Charlotte, Augusta, Elizabeth, Mary, Sophia, and Amelia, the youngest.

While the king's sons went out into the world as they grew older, his six daughters remained at home. The queen was given a sum of money every year, some of which she spent on her daughters. She was in charge of the lives and education of the girls.

Most of the young princesses' days were spent with the queen. They took walks, practiced needlepoint, and read. For fun, they gave card parties, visited theaters and attended concerts, and held occasional balls. It was the typical life of upper-class ladies of the day.

The family took vacations together several times each year. Sometimes they went sailing off the coast of England. For the royal family, life was full of luxury. But they also had many duties to perform. They were expected to spend many hours a day in public service.

The king loved the company of his daughters and wanted them to stay single. Only three of George's daughters ever married: Princess

Charlotte married at age 31; Princess Elizabeth was 48 when she married; and Princess Mary had her wedding when she was 40. None of George's married daughters had children that lived past infancy.

George liked life in the country as a gentleman farmer. He wanted to be an example to the nation of what a farmer could do with the land. He drained a wilderness of swampland and built two model farms. George introduced merino sheep from Spain and made other improvements.

Following his instructions, workers planted new crops on his farms and used better plows. When the threshing machine was invented in 1784, it was soon used on the king's farms. His farms became a popular tourist attraction.

George became known as "Farmer George" in the newspapers of the day. He was delighted with the nickname. George sometimes contributed articles on his farming experiments to a magazine named *Annals of Agriculture.* They appeared under the name of his shepherd at Windsor Castle, Ralph Robinson. Most people knew that the king had written the articles. He always carried the latest issue of the magazine with him when he traveled. His good example led other noblemen to also establish up-to-date farms and herds of cattle for breeding superior stock.

Hunting was the king's favorite hobby. He would have liked to hunt all day long until there was no more light. But the queen wanted him to be home for dinner. So every day that he was in the country, George would leave the house after breakfast and return about 4 o'clock in the afternoon. That would make him just on time for the family dinner.

George was also dedicated to physical fitness. On the regular journeys of the royal family, the king rode on horseback while the rest of the family rode in coaches. Much later in his life, at the age of 66, he rode 10 miles on horseback through a thunderstorm just to keep a dinner engagement.

A fox hunt in the country. George loved to hunt all day but always tried to be home in time for dinner with the queen.

The king was not only dedicated to exercise, he also ate very little food and chose what he ate carefully. His dinner in the afternoon was soup, a meat course, one vegetable, and fruit. His favorite meal was mutton (lamb) with turnips or beets. The family always ate roast beef on Sundays.

With his meal, George would drink several glasses of wine. He often mixed the wine with water. He never drank anything stronger. Around 7 o'clock in the evening, the king and queen usually hosted tea. The family and visitors gathered for conversation and a light snack.

They would play card games and talk until about 10 o'clock. Then the king and queen would host another meal, which they called supper. They went to bed around 11 o'clock. Every once in a while they might stay up until midnight. The king and queen had separate apartments connected by a private staircase. But they slept together in the king's room.

The entire royal family loved music. George played the harpsichord, flute, and piano. He may also have played the organ. Both the king and the queen sponsored bands. Each played and sang with their bands. The king especially loved the music of George Handel.

George still loved books. He had a huge collection of them. In 1762, he bought 32,000 books. They were all about the English Civil War, during which forces led by Oliver Cromwell overthrew the monarchy, and the time called the Protectorate, when Cromwell ruled England. In 1765, George purchased a collection of early printed books. They cost more than 10,000 pounds. That would be more than $100,000 today.

Every year, George spent a lot of money at book auctions all over Europe. When he died, his library contained 65,000 books. It included more than 200 Bibles and many of the early works of William Shakespeare.

In buying these books, George was forming a national library. He ordered its keepers to allow anyone to use the books in the royal collection. He didn't want people who disagreed with him to be kept from learning.

While George liked to lead his everyday life as a gentleman farmer, he was still the ruler of the greatest empire on earth. In 1757, the British defeated the French in India and took control of that rich area of the world. Great Britain

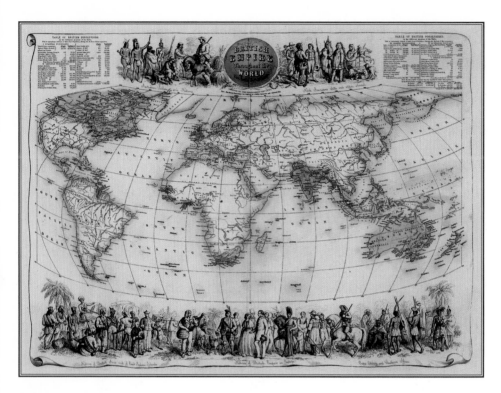

An early map of the British Empire throughout the world. Areas in red were ruled by King George III in the 1700s.

also controlled areas in Africa and the West Indies. Its merchant fleet and navy controlled the oceans of the world.

When George came to the throne, Great Britain was in another war with France called the Seven Years' War (1756–1763). The fighting in North America was called the French and Indian

War. When Great Britain won that war, the French were kicked out. All of Canada and the territory within the present United States from the Mississippi River to the Atlantic Ocean became British **colonies**.

George believed that it was his duty to preserve the British Empire. He also thought he should do everything he could to make it even bigger. But people in the American colonies didn't agree with him. They were beginning to think they'd be better off not being ruled by Great Britain.

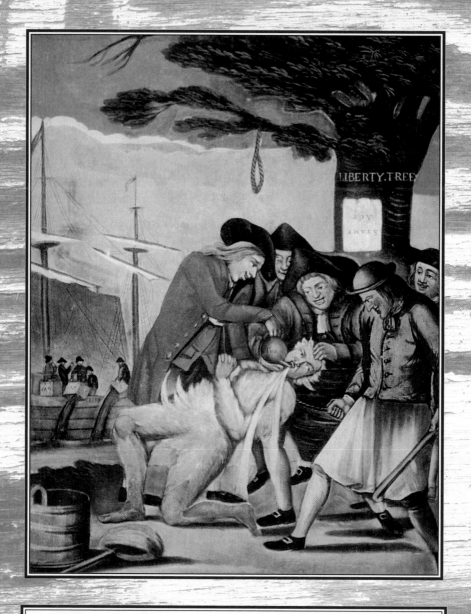

To protest England's tax on tea, American patriots force a kettle of tea down the throat of a British tax collector, whom they have also tarred and feathered. Taxation would be one of the major causes of the Revolutionary War.

Losing
a War

Although the victory over France in the Seven Years' War greatly extended the British Empire through the addition of the vast lands of Canada, Great Britain had borrowed a lot of money to fight the war. Now Great Britain found itself with a debt of 130 million pounds. And gaining all that land meant that the British needed even more money, to set up new governments in Canada and pay soldiers to protect these new colonies.

The British government decided that it wanted the colonies to contribute 100,000 pounds. That money would help pay for the British army in North

America. British subjects at home already paid high **taxes,** and they liked the idea of making the colonists help to pay for the soldiers. From 1763 to the beginning of the American **Revolution**, Parliament did just what the British public wanted. The House of Commons passed a series of laws creating new taxes for the colonists.

The colonists got very angry. No colonists sat in the House of Commons. They felt that it was wrong for them to have no say about the laws they would have to obey.

For years, the colonists in America had paid no taxes. It was a part of English tradition that no one could be taxed by Parliament if they did not have a representative in Parliament. Many people in America claimed that since the colonists had no representatives, they could not be taxed.

Then, Parliament passed the Sugar Act. This law taxed French **molasses**. Americans used molasses to make rum to sell in Europe. But with the added tax, it became too expensive for Americans to make rum.

The Sugar Act also created changes in how Americans could trade their products with other nations. Every ship with goods for trade that left America had to first stop in England for inspections before it could go to any other nation in Europe. This made American products cost much more than British products.

Smugglers and others who broke the law went to trial. But they were tried by a judge instead of a jury, which also made many colonists angry. The people who lived in England had the right to a trial by jury. The colonists believed they should have the same right.

The Sugar Act hurt New England most. More trading was done from those colonies than from the other American colonies. But the law didn't raise as much money as Parliament had hoped. All it did was make the colonists angry.

Great Britain still needed more money. So, in 1765, Parliament passed another tax on the American colonies. This tax hurt almost everyone. Called the Stamp Act, it said that all legal and

Benjamin Franklin (left, standing) represented the American colonies at a special meeting with King George III and his court.

business documents had to be written on paper that had been stamped by a government office.

The government collected money every time someone bought a stamped piece of paper. This happened when people bought newspapers, got a license, bought a piece of land, or drew up a will.

Leaders of the American colonies protested

to Parliament. The British government didn't pay any attention to them.

Patrick Henry made a fiery speech in the Virginia legislature. He said that taxation without representation was **tyranny**. Word of the speech quickly spread around the colonies, and many people agreed with him.

The people of Boston decided to do something to show how they felt. They closed the courts and flew their flags at half-mast, which symbolizes that people have lost something or someone they value. They also refused to load and unload ships in the harbor. It was one of the most important harbors in the colonies.

George thought the colonists were wrong. The government helped British colonists all around the world. George believed that Parliament had the right to tax the colonists, who had benefited from Great Britain's protection. He wasn't concerned with the size of the taxes. He simply wanted everyone to understand that the king had rights. One of those rights was to tax all of his subjects. His grandfather and other kings of England had had this right. George thought it was his job to keep this right for future kings.

But the Stamp Act didn't work and didn't raise much money. It actually hurt business in Great Britain because Americans stopped trading with British companies. Lord Grenville was in charge of the **treasury**. He had come up with all the laws that the colonists didn't like. So George fired Grenville, and in March 1766, Parliament decided to get rid of the Stamp Act.

The news reached Boston on May 16. People drank toasts to the health of King George III. But Parliament did not want the colonists to think that they had won their battle against taxes. So it passed the Declaratory Act. This law stated that Parliament had the right to tax the colonists.

One year later, George chose Charles Townshend to be in charge of the British treasury. Townshend wanted to solve the old problem of how to raise money to pay for the British soldiers in America.

Patrick Henry delivers a fiery speech to Virginia legislators against unfair British taxation.

The colonists had used many arguments when they protested the Stamp Act. One problem, they said, was that it was unfair for Parliament to collect taxes for business that was conducted only in the colonies. Parliament had agreed with them. But Townshend thought it would be fair to collect taxes on goods that came to the colonies from outside North America. Townshend's Revenue Act of 1767 said colonists would to have to pay taxes on glass, paint, lead, paper, and tea. These were things the colonists needed but couldn't make for themselves in America yet.

Townshend wanted to use some of the money he collected from these taxes to pay the salaries of colonial governors and other officials. In the past, colonial **legislatures** had paid these people. Sometimes they had refused to pay a governor or official who would not do what they wanted. Townshend hoped to take control of the governors away from colonists.

Just like the acts before it, the Townshend Act never collected a lot of money. The colonists simply stopped bringing in British goods that were taxed. This caused a huge drop in trade between the British and the colonies. Parliament could see that the colonists were serious about not paying British taxes.

In 1770, George chose a new person to lead the British government. The new **prime minister** was his boyhood friend, Frederick North. Lord North, as he now was called, agreed with the king about the American colonies. Both men saw that the hated taxes were doing no good. But they wanted to show that they had a right to tax the colonists. On March 5, 1770, they got rid of all the Townshend Acts except for the tax on tea.

Colonists loved drinking tea. They did not want to do without their favorite drink. So they began to buy large amounts of Dutch tea that was being smuggled into the colonies.

In May 1773, Parliament passed the Tea Act. This law cut the price of British tea almost in half. The tea now cost much less than the illegally smuggled Dutch tea. But there was a catch: the British tea still had a small tax on it.

The British government thought that the colonists would give in and pay the tax in order to get cheaper tea. They were wrong.

On the night of December 16, 1773, about 150 **patriots** dressed up as American Indians and boarded three British ships in Boston. The men found more than 300 chests of British tea and dumped them into the harbor.

The British were angry. George said Boston had to be punished. Boston Harbor was closed to all ships, and more soldiers were sent to patrol the Massachusetts colony. Many people thought war would come soon.

On September 5, 1774, the first Continental Congress met in Philadelphia. The most important leaders from 12 of the 13 American colonies tried to find a way

In England, George III was a popular man. People liked and respected him.

In the American colonies, it was a different matter. George was seen as a bully. People thought he was an evil man who always wanted to have his own way. American colonists called him names and made jokes about him.

After the Revolutionary War ended, the leaders of the new nation discussed what type of government Americans needed. One thing almost everyone agreed on was that the United States must never be ruled by a king. They insisted that their leader be chosen by the people.

General Gage, commander of British troops at the Battles of Lexington and Concord. The fighting there marked the beginning of the Revolutionary War.

to solve their problems with Great Britain. It was hard to find a solution without going to war.

The following spring, General Thomas Gage, the British governor of Massachusetts, took action of his own. He discovered that the colonists had hidden guns at Lexington and Concord and sent troops to take them. No one knows who fired first, but a battle broke out. The day's fighting ended with American patriots chasing the British troops back to Boston. Around 50 patriots and perhaps 75 British soldiers died on the battlefield.

In May, Ethan Allen and his Green Mountain Boys overran the British fort at Ticonderoga, New York. Soon nearly 16,000 colonists surrounded the 10,000 British soldiers in Boston. At the Battle of Bunker Hill on June 17, the British forces suffered more than 225 men dead and 825 wounded.

It took six weeks for the news of the Battles of Lexington and Concord to reach London. When George heard the news, he wanted to punish the colonists. He issued a formal **decree**. It said that the colonies were in rebellion.

Several of the king's advisors warned him that he could never defeat the colonists in their own lands. Great Britain was trying to fight a war 3,000 miles away and it took three to six months for supplies to reach North America.

They told the king that the best thing to do was

block the American ports. The colonists wouldn't be able to beat the mighty British navy. And without shipping, the colonists wouldn't get the goods they needed to survive. After some time, the colonies would have to beg for forgiveness.

George would not listen. He could be stubborn, and he was set on bringing the colonists to their knees. He sent three additional army generals– William Howe, John Burgoyne, and Charles Cornwallis–to help Gage defeat the Americans.

Over the next three years, Great Britain sent thousands of soldiers to fight in the colonies. In August 1775, five groups of soldiers from Hanover were taken into the British army by the king. Other German soldiers were also hired. In all, Germany sent more than 30,000 additional troops to the colonies during the war. In America, they were called Hessians because many were from the small kingdom of Hesse-Cassel. More than 5,000 of these paid soldiers **deserted** and remained in America after the war.

Most of the British people thought their army

would quickly defeat the colonies. But on July 4, 1776, the colonies declared their independence from Great Britain. The new country asked France, Holland, and Spain–three old enemies of England's–for help.

George and his generals made a new plan, still hoping to defeat the colonists. General Howe would capture Philadelphia. Then he would march his army north to meet General Burgoyne. Burgoyne would march south from Canada along the Hudson River. If this plan were successful, it would split the colonies in two.

Howe's superior forces soundly defeated the **rebel** army under the command of General Washington at Brandywine Creek. He then went on to capture Philadelphia. Burgoyne began his march from Canada and quickly captured Fort Ticonderoga. But Howe didn't start marching to meet Burgoyne right away.

That pause provided all the time that the colonists needed. In September and October of 1777, more than 20,000 Americans defeated a

Patriots pulled down the statue of King George III in New York City after the Declaration of Independence was read.

smaller British army in two battles near the village of Saratoga, New York. Burgoyne was forced to surrender all his men. Without Burgoyne's support, Howe was forced to leave Philadelphia.

The American victory at Saratoga was important. France had been wondering whether it should help the American colonists. After the battle, the French believed that the colonies had a chance to win. Early the next spring, France recognized the United States of America, then broke off relations with Great Britain and started helping the American colonies.

This gave King George a new problem. France was just across the narrow English Channel from England. George had to make sure the English coast was safe.

Two years after France began supporting the United States, Spain joined the war, also on the American side. Then Holland sided with the United States in 1780.

By then, George really had his hands full. His armies were fighting the colonists in America. They were also fighting the French in India, Africa, Canada, and the West Indies. And they were fighting the Spanish in Central America, Florida, the West Indies, and Gibraltar. In addition there were the battles against the Dutch in Ceylon, the East Indies, and the North Sea.

Lord North, the king's old friend, still felt that Great Britain could not win the war with the colonists. Most of the members of Parliament agreed. North did not want to go on under these conditions and asked George to dismiss him from his office.

George refused. He did not want to be the king who had lost a part of the British Empire. But everything was going wrong.

In October 1781, Cornwallis and his 6,000 troops were trapped in Virginia by General Washington's army of more than 8,000, who were aided by an additional 7,800 French troops. The British were surrounded and began to run low on food and ammunition. On October 17, Cornwallis agreed to surrender his entire army at Yorktown, Virginia.

George ignored the reports about Yorktown. In his heart, though, he knew that the defeat would mean the end of the war in America.

When North heard the news, he shouted, "Oh God! It is all over." Less than a year later, North simply could not take it any longer and resigned.

The colonial army's victory at the Battle of Yorktown marked the end of the Revolutionary War.

Other members of the House of Commons lost their elections. They were replaced by members of Parliament more friendly to the United States.

On March 5, 1782, a law was introduced that allowed the king to talk with the rebels. That April, Benjamin Franklin told the British that if they wanted to end the war in America, they also had to end their war with France, Spain, and Holland. Parliament and the king agreed. Talks to create a peace treaty began in Paris in June 1782. The signing of the Treaty of Paris in 1783 formally marked the end to the war.

George felt that he had failed to live up to the duty of a British king. The American Revolution was the only war that England had lost since 1707. The king knew that his people were disappointed. He thought of giving up his position as king. He even wrote two drafts of a speech in which he admitted that his attempt to rule the country had been unsuccessful. But in the end, George decided to remain as king.

William Pitt took over as prime minister after North resigned. (He was called William Pitt the Younger so people wouldn't confuse him with his father, who had also been a prime minister.) With George's support, Pitt saw Britain through the difficult times ahead.

George in later life. When he was 50 years old, George got a mysterious illness that made him sick for many years.

4

Hard Times

Geooge and the British people enjoyed the peace after the war had ended. The king kept out of politics. He simply did his royal jobs. He enjoyed his life in the country. But George still had a problem. His sons kept spending too much money and getting into other trouble.

Then things got worse. In the summer of 1788, while George was on vacation, he got a terrible pain in his stomach. It took five weeks for him to get better.

The ailing **monarch** went home to Windsor Castle to rest. Instead, he got worse. His walk was unsteady. He started talking all the time. He spoke of seeing and doing impossible things. Sometimes George walked around mumbling, and then he started to drool. People began to talk about the king's behavior. The king's doctors thought that he had lost his mind. It was scary to see a king act this way.

In November 1788, George was taken away from Windsor Castle and put in the Prince of Wales's home at Kew. The king had to be restrained with a **straitjacket**. Everyone believed that the Prince of Wales would have to take over the king's duties.

No one knew what had made George so sick. Today it is believed that George had an illness called porphyria. This disease comes from having too much copper in the body. It makes urine turn a reddish color. Like George, people with porphyria see things that aren't there. They lose sleep and have rashes on their bodies. The disease also makes people nervous and twitchy. People with porphyria now take medicine to make them feel better. But no one knew about the disease in 1789.

George thought he was insane. So did his family and the members of Parliament. Even the common people thought their king had gone mad. Over the winter, George gradually got better. By April of 1789, he was so much better that a thanksgiving service was held in his honor at St. Paul's Church in London.

A few weeks after that service, revolution broke out in France. On July 14, 1789, mobs of poor Frenchmen freed the prisoners held in the Bastille, a big prison in Paris. The king and queen of France were taken captive. They were executed four years later.

The French people started a new government. On February 1, 1793, the new government of France declared war on Great Britain and Holland. The British would fight the French on and off for the next 22 years.

George believed that it was his moral duty to fight. He wrote in 1794 that the war with France was something "that every tie of religion, morality and society not only authorises but demands."

King Louis XVI of France is taken prisoner by revolutionaries. After the King's execution, the French government declared war on Great Britain.

But he did not fight just for moral reasons. The French promised that they would cut the head off any country's king if the people rioted

Warships in a naval battle. France and England were at war on and off for 22 years near the end of George's reign.

to show that they wanted a new government. George and the other nobles in England wanted to survive. They joined nearly half a million Englishmen in being ready to fight the French.

During the 1790s, the king was in good health and high spirits. In a letter from March 1791, his daughter Augusta wrote of George, "It would do your heart as much good as it does mine . . . to see him come home from a late day at St. James's or a long hunt, the least fatigued of the party and always so good-humoured and cheerful."

George's illness had changed his personality. He was more gentle, quiet, and friendly.

One problem that faced the king and Parliament at this time involved Ireland, the large island located just west of Britain. In 1782, Parliament had given Ireland some independence. The Irish were granted the right to be ruled by their own legislature. But an official appointed by the king was given the right to veto any laws that Ireland's government passed. And only Protestants, who were a small part of Ireland's population, were allowed to vote.

As the years passed, the Catholic population of Ireland seemed more and more likely to rebel. And France had promised to come to their aid.

George and the English nobles worried. What if France decided to help Ireland? Would the French try to kill George and England's other leaders?

Finally, Prime Minister Pitt came up with an idea. If Ireland would agree to be ruled by Parliament, all Irish Catholic men would be able to vote and hold office. The government would pay all members of the clergy, not just those who belonged to the Church of England.

George refused to agree. He felt such action would make him break the promise he had made when he was crowned king. His coronation oath included a promise to maintain the rights of the Protestant Church of England. George thought those rights would be weakened if he gave Catholics a role in government.

The problems between Ireland and England weren't solved.

Windsor Castle, home to kings and queens of England for hundreds of years. When George was sick, Queen Charlotte took care of him in a small apartment in the castle.

The End

George got sick again on February 13, 1801. His condition kept getting worse until ten days later he lay all night in a coma. He was so sick that everybody thought he was going to die.

A week later, George surprised them all. He woke up and was very calm. He asked where he was and how long he had been sick.

But he soon got sick yet again. And again he awoke feeling perfectly healthy. He visited with the queen the next day. The day after that, he started thinking about politics. George asked what had been happening in Parliament. He met with his ministers on March 17.

When the king wanted to appear in public again, his doctors got nervous. So they kidnapped him and took him to a secluded house at Kew. No one was allowed to visit him.

This treatment made George very angry. Finally, he told his doctors that unless they allowed him to see his wife and family, he would no longer sign any official papers. If the king stopped signing papers, the country would stop working. The doctors agreed to do what George asked.

George carried on his royal duties. And the doctors continued to treat him. But everyone worried that the king might become "insane" again at any moment.

By 1804, George looked very pale and painfully thin. His mind remained clear, but his eyesight had begun to fail. He could no longer see across a room.

On October 25, 1810, the country celebrated

George's 50th year on the throne. He remained very popular with the English people. On the other hand, the princes were very unpopular. They continued to run up large debts and behave badly in public.

On the day of George's 50th anniversary celebration, he caught a cold. For the remainder of his life, he would be ill.

He had been staying with Princess Amelia, his favorite and youngest daughter, while she was very sick. When she died, George was heartbroken.

In January 1811, Parliament was so concerned about the king's condition that it passed a bill of **regency**. The bill put the queen in charge of George's care. She made arrangements for him to live in a small apartment in Windsor Castle. Parliament made the Prince of Wales his regent. That meant that George's son would rule the British Empire in his place.

By the summer, George's illness had gotten much worse. His mind wandered and he talked wildly. He could never seem to sleep, even when given powerful drugs. Often he became so violent that he had to be kept in a straitjacket. He stopped taking care of himself and his hair and beard grew long and white.

George no longer asked about his family, though the queen still went to see him. Almost no one else, except for his doctors, visited the king. Servants and guards cared for him.

In 1818, the queen died. Then George's second son, the duke of York, became responsible for making decisions about his care. In November 1819, George's health got even worse. He became even weaker and thinner.

King George III died on January 29, 1820. His body lay in state for two days, with lines of people walking by to get a last glimpse of their longtime king. He was buried in St. George's Chapel on February 16, 1820. Thousands of mourners went to the burial site.

Very few English people could remember

King George IV, George's oldest son. The people criticized him for being irresponsible and spending too much money.

any other king. George III had ruled for 60 years. For the most part, his people loved and respected him.

Two things had guided George's actions. He had worked to preserve what he considered good. And he also wanted to protect his subjects, the British people. His popularity had saved British royalty during a time of wars and conflict. A less popular man might have brought an end to the British royal family.

GLOSSARY

baptized–to be given a Christian name during a church ceremony

cathedral–a large church and the center of the church leaders' power

colony–a territory owned and ruled by a distant country

court–the place where a king lives

decree–an official legal order

desert–to leave the armed forces without permission

earl–an inherited title representing ownership of land and estates

empire–a group of nations governed by one ruler

House of Commons–the lower house in the English Parliament, whose members are elected

House of Lords–the upper house in the English Parliament, whose members are lords, high-ranking nobles who inherit their seats in the government

legislature–a group of people in the government who make laws

molasses–a thick, black syrup taken from unrefined sugar and used to make rum

monarch–a king or queen

noble–a person with an inherited, high-ranking title such as a duke or duchess

patriots–American colonists who believed the colonies should be independent from Britain

Parliament–the British legislature, which is composed of the House of Lords and the House of Commons and which makes the country's laws

prime minister–the highest-ranking government official in England, who was formerly appointed by the king or queen

rebel–a person who resists authority, wanting to overthrow laws or a government

regency–a time during which someone rules in a king or queen's place

revolution–a war fought to overthrow an old government and establish a new one

straitjacket–a jacket made of heavy material, with sleeves so long that they can be wrapped around and tied behind the wearer, making it impossible for him or her to move

taxes–money paid by people to support their government

treasury–the government department that is in charge of a country's money

tutor–a private teacher

tyranny–severe, harsh power shown by a government or ruler

CHRONOLOGY

1738   George William Frederick is born on June 4 in London, England.

1751   Father dies.

1760   King George II dies; George III becomes king of Great Britain.

1761   Marries Charlotte Sophia of Mecklenburg; officially crowned King George III of Great Britain.

1762   Son George, the Prince of Wales and future King George IV, is born.

1765   The Stamp Act takes effect in America.

1773   The Boston Tea Party takes place in Boston Harbor.

1775   The Battles of Lexington and Concord and Bunker Hill are fought near Boston; the war between Great Britain and the American colonies begins.

1776   American colonies declare independence on July 4.

1777   The British are defeated at Saratoga; General Burgoyne surrenders.

1781   American army wins the battle of Yorktown; General Charles Cornwallis surrenders; the fighting ends.

1783   The Treaty of Paris is signed, officially ending the war.

1785	Great Britain recognizes America as an independent country; King George III meets the U.S. minister to Great Britain.
1788	George's first serious illness occurs.
1789	The French Revolution begins.
1810	George suffers another illness.
1811	The regency period is declared; the Prince of Wales rules in his father's place.
1820	George dies on January 29.

REVOLUTIONARY WAR TIME LINE ⸺

1765   The Stamp Act is passed by the British. Violent protests against it break out in the colonies.

1766   Britain ends the Stamp Act.

1767   Britain passes a law that taxes glass, painter's lead, paper, and tea in the colonies.

1770   Five colonists are killed by British soldiers in the Boston Massacre.

1773   People are angry about the taxes on tea. They throw boxes of tea from ships in Boston Harbor into the water. It ruins the tea. The event is called the Boston Tea Party.

1774   The British pass laws to punish Boston for the Boston Tea Party. They close Boston Harbor. Leaders in the colonies meet to plan a response to these actions.

1775   The Battles of Lexington and Concord begin the American Revolution.

1776   The Declaration of Independence is signed. France and Spain give money to help the Americans fight Britain. Nathan Hale is captured by the British. He is charged with being a spy and is executed.

1777   Leaders choose a flag for America. The American troops win some important battles over the British. General Washington and his troops spend a very cold, hungry winter in Valley Forge.

1778 France sends ships to help the Americans win the war. The British are forced to leave Philadelphia.

1779 French ships head back to France. The French support the Americans in other ways.

1780 Americans discover that Benedict Arnold is a traitor. He escapes to the British. Major battles take place in North and South Carolina.

1781 The British surrender at Yorktown.

1783 A peace treaty is signed in France. British troops leave New York.

1787 The U.S. Constitution is written. Delaware becomes the first state in the Union.

1789 George Washington becomes the first president. John Adams is vice president.

FURTHER READING

Ashley, Mike. *The Mammoth Book of British Kings and Queens.* New York: Carroll & Graf Publishers, 1998.

Cannon, John, and Ralph Griffiths. *The Oxford Illustrated History of the British Monarchy.* New York: Oxford University Press, 1988.

Hakim, Joy. *From Colonies to Country.* New York: Oxford University Press, 1993.

Rosenburg, John. *First in War: George Washington in the American Revolution.* Brookfield, Conn.: Millbrook, 1998.

Rubel, David. *Scholastic Encyclopedia of the Presidents and Their Times.* New York: Scholastic, 1994.

Strong, Roy. *The Story of Britain.* New York: Fromm International Publishing Corporation, 1996.

INDEX

PICTURE CREDITS

page

3: National Archives
6: New Millennium Images
11: The Library of Congress
13: The Library of Congress
14: The Library of Congress
18: The Library of Congress
22: The Library of Congress
25: The Library of Congress
27: The Library of Congress
31: New Millennium Images
34: The Library of Congress

36: National Archives
40: National Archives
43: National Archives
47: The Library of Congress
51: National Archives
54 New Millennium Images
56: The Library of Congress
60: National Archives
61: New Millennium Images
64: New Millennium Images
69: The Library of Congress

ABOUT THE AUTHOR

ANN GRAHAM GAINES is a freelance author and photo researcher who lives in the woods near Gonzales, Texas, with her four children.

Senior Consulting Editor **ARTHUR M. SCHLESINGER, JR.** is the leading American historian of our time. He won the Pulitzer Prize for his book *The Age of Jackson* (1945), and again for *A Thousand Days* (1965). This chronicle of the Kennedy Administration also won a National Book Award. He has written many other books, including a multi-volume series, *The Age of Roosevelt.* Professor Schlesinger is the Albert Schweitzer Professor of the Humanities at the City University of New York, and has been involved in several other Chelsea House projects, including the COLONIAL LEADERS series of biographies on the most prominent figures of early American history.